Elizabeth A. Weber

A Beautiful Mourning

iUniverse, Inc.
New York   Bloomington

iUniverse books may be ordered through booksellers or by contacting:

iUniverse
1663 Liberty Drive
Bloomington, IN 47403
www.iuniverse.com
1-800-Authors (1-800-288-4677)

Because of the dynamic nature of the Internet, any Web addresses or
links contained in this book may have changed since publication and
may no longer be valid. The views expressed in this work are solely those
of the author and do not necessarily reflect the views of the publisher,
and the publisher hereby disclaims any responsibility for them.

ISBN: 978-1-4502-2817-6 (sc)
ISBN: 978-1-4502-2818-3 (ebook)

Printed in the United States of America

iUniverse rev. date: 04/26/2010

For all those who mourn.

The cloud weeps, and then the garden sprouts.
The baby cries, and the mother's milk flows.
The nurse of Creation has said, Let them cry a lot.

This rain-weeping and sun-burning twine together
to make us grow. Keep your intelligence white-hot
and your grief glistening, so your life will stay fresh.
Cry easily like a little child.

Rumi

Acknowledgements

I would like to express my deepest gratitude to Inayat Khan whose words have been "sown on the soil" of my heart and have grown to become the living garden in which I dwell.

A special thanks to Reverend Chad O'Shea for his humor and wisdom and the Unity Prayer Chaplain training. Thanks to Carol McCleland Ph.D. for her inspired "Seasons of Change" work. Also, Hiyagua Cohen for her compassionate coaching in my darkest hour.

A heartfelt thanks to the members of my Women's Writing Circle: Anita Linn, Ariel Stephanie Marsh, and Marilyn Mueller. Thanks for the encouraging feedback on my manuscript from my dearest friends Sura Sheldon, Rabia Longworth, Aftab Beckett, and Gayatri Hull.

Much love to my beloved Terry Lee, Donarose and Roger Rompel, and my darling son, Jared Siems. My sincere thanks to Cathy Truehart for the wonderful title of this book, Lynn Yanis for her astute editing, and Coleman Barks for his generous permission to reprint the poem "The Cloud Weeps." And my deep appreciation goes out to all the authors whose words inspired me throughout my journey.

Out of a consideration for privacy, some names have been changed in this memoir.

Contents

Chapter 1

An Ancestral Sorrow

I heard the words, "Mourn not over the death of the Beloved ..." and suddenly my mind reeled. Mourn not? You can ask anything of me, I thought, but not this. That's when the full impact of my loss hit me with all the power of a tsunami wave.

Up until that point, my husband's memorial service had been so festive that it was more like a wedding than a funeral. I remember myself at the front door of the church welcoming people with all the gaiety of a mother-of-the-bride. It was so heartwarming to see long-lost friends and family. And what could be more celebratory than honoring a life well-lived? But now I plunge down from my euphoria with a dizzying speed and the floodgates of my sorrow burst open with an unstoppable force.

This is the point of no return, where all roads seemed to converge. I cry for myself and I cry for all humanity. I cry from an ancestral well of sorrow. I cry what I call the "ugly cry." I had only seen snapshots of this type of grief. The grief we all immediately recognize from the newspapers. The grief that shows on the face of women from war-ravaged lands or on the mother after her honor-roll student is taken from her in a drive-by shooting. We don't have to read the news story's caption because the face says it all. It requires no translation.

Here I am in a quiet, suburban church gasping for breath, choking, and wailing like there is no tomorrow because in this moment there is no tomorrow. It is the end of my life as I had known it. And it is here in my darkest hour that I have my first glimmer of the beauty that awaits me. In my exposed and trembling state, I feel the hearts of every person in that church leap up to join me. It is as though I am carried by the loving intentions that leap out of my fellow mourners' hearts.

If someone were observing this from the outside all they would have seen is a woman looking very alone in a church pew. But from the inside of this experience it is as if I can feel the love of every person gathered around me and carrying me through this dark passage. It is a tangible experience of being held by prayer. This is the first surprise on my mourning journey: When I was too weak to walk this journey on my own, I found that I didn't have to. All I had to do was show up and embrace the moment honestly.

This journey of embracing my mourning process is what this book is all about. It may have been the most courageous thing I've ever done. And I don't know why but it seems that taking this journey was my destiny. Maybe because being weak was never my strong suit. Maybe like most North Americans, I've been indoctrinated to believe we are rugged individualists who "pick ourselves up by the bootstraps." We "suck in our gut" and keep "a stiff upper lip" as we press on.

For whatever reason, I knew at that moment that this mourning process would be something that I wouldn't turn my back on. I will follow my inner calling to "be still and know that I am God." (Psalm 46:10) When people ask me, "What will you do? Where will you go?" I know with absolute unshakable certainty that I am not going to do anything. It is time to be. And I will be with this mourning process fully.

Chapter 2

Destined for a Fall

Several months before my husband Bob died, we spent a tender afternoon with his daughters filling out his Living Will. This document put into writing his wishes about his medical care and memorial service. Bob spoke, and his oldest daughter Mary acted as the scribe. And it was my delight in creating a memorial service that would do Bob justice that kept me in the initial euphoria I felt during his service.

Bob was the most naturally kind and good man I have ever known. But this book is not about Bob's wonderful life—it's about how hard it was to lose him. We all know the saying, you don't know what you've got 'til it's gone. Well, I knew what I had. I entered our relationship at age forty after spending my entire adult life working my way through community college, college, and graduate school while being a single parent. By the time I met Bob, I was clearly my own woman. He was the most extraordinary man I had ever come across, but Bob had just turned sixty-five. As Shakespeare might have said, "Ay, there's the rub."

Bob was freshly retired when we met, and he was eager to live life to its fullest. But I couldn't enter into a relationship with him without my eyes being wide open to the possibility—the probability—that I would lose him. Paradoxically, this made every moment of our lives together deliciously sweet. We were so in love we made other people swoon just looking at us.

I remember one time when we were getting a cart at one of our favorite grocery stores, a woman pulled us aside to talk. She excitedly told us that she had been driving behind us on the 101 freeway for the last twenty miles. She gushed about how she had never seen two people more in love and what a pleasure that was and how it made her day. We blushed and thanked her and continued on with our shopping. Later I wondered how anyone would know that the couple in the car in front of them was in love?

The only thing is, the bigger the love—the harder the fall.

Chapter 3

Another Dark Passage

I elect to be the one to fly to California and hold the memorial service there, rather than asking Bob's large extended family to pay the expenses of flying to North Carolina where he passed away. When I return home, however, I have to travel through my second dark passage. I have to get off the plane and walk through the airport with no one to greet me.

When Bob and I lived on the breathtakingly beautiful island of Kauai, I often traveled to the Big Island for trainings for my work as a therapist. Bob drove me to the airport in the morning and picked me up in the evening.

The first time Bob picked me up he swept me off my feet by greeting me with the traditional flower lei. I had only been gone for a day. But—as any woman would—I loved it! The beautiful and touching thing was that Bob greeted me with a flower lei not just the first time I returned home from the Big Island, but also the second, the third, the fourth, the fifth ... and the twentieth.

Bob greeted me as if my coming home from a day at work was a grand homecoming. With his beautiful blue eyes sparkling, he told me I was a treasure he adored. For ten years, I had been deeply and truly loved by my darling of a husband. But now, I walk through the cavernous airport alone, with no one waiting for me. The only sound I hear is the lonely echo of my own footfalls.

My days of flower leis and Garden Islands are over. My days of loving and being loved are over. I return home alone and the home I return to is part of this story.

Bob and I had been volunteering at a holistic retreat center in upstate New York that summer, and had agreed to housesit for one of his sons in North Carolina when our summer commitment ended. After Bob died, I had to return to a house that was not a home. The house was bought as an investment property and was brand new. It held no history, warmth, or happy memories. It was simply an empty house. To make matters worse, it was part of a new housing development that had been hastily built by demolishing all the existing trees. The landscape resembled a moonscape more than a welcoming neighborhood.

In this stark house, I am without family, friends, church, or work. And, of course, I am without the best thing in my life—my beloved husband. Here is where I will mourn. Fortunately, I will not mourn entirely alone.

Chapter 4

A Crowd of Sorrows

About two months before Bob actually died I came to my first crossroads. I had to squarely face the fact that Bob might die. Despite my fervent longings for him to recover, I had to acknowledge that, in truth, this may be Bob's time of passing. If it was, I would need to change my position from being the eternal optimist to being one who steps back and allows a gracious death.

I thought about what a terrible burden it would be to leave this world feeling as if you're letting someone down. I needed to find the inner poise to continue to believe in the miracle of healing, and accept that if this was his time to die—then as the Native Americans used to say— "it's a good day to die!"

My final act of love for Bob would be the act of letting him go. Since we were so close there was no way for me to put on a false face so I needed to find the strength to let him know that I would be okay. In his poem "Guesthouse" the Sufi poet Rumi implores us to welcome in each experience in life as a valued guest; even if they are a "crowd of sorrows that have come to sweep us clean." And so I would do this.

I would meet each phase of this journey and embrace it, but I knew that I couldn't do it alone. I would have to face losing the love of my life, finding a new home, and finding work. I compassionately recognized this would be too much for anyone to handle alone, so I determined to get the help I will need and take it one step at a time. As the famed mythologist Joseph Campbell outlined in his description of "The Hero's Journey," when a man or woman agrees to "Answer the Call" in life and go through "The Supreme Ordeal," they will often find guides or mentors along the way. The guide cannot take the journey for you…but they can point the way.

It happened to be the week of Thanksgiving when I made the inner commitment to reach out to someone. I didn't know who that would be or how it would manifest; I just knew that I would do it.

About two or three days later, I received a bulk email from an acquaintance I had met while living on the island of Kauai. Her name was Sequoia and her email said that she was returning to school to get her Ph.D. in Human Development and Life Coaching. She was looking for someone going through a major life-transition, as she wanted to offer pro-bono coaching as part of her studies.

I wrote back pleading for her help and to my great relief she agreed. She regretted that her program wouldn't be starting until February so she couldn't help until then, but she assured me she would be holding me tenderly in her heart.

As it turned out, Bob passed away on January 23rd, and I went to California for the memorial service at the beginning of February. Mercifully, by the time I return to my painfully empty life, Sequoia is waiting for me.

Chapter 5

❦

Winter

Sequoia is studying a form of coaching called *The Seasons of Change*. This approach was created by Carol McClelland, Ph.D. and is described in her book of the same title with the subtitle: *Using Nature's Wisdom to Grow through Life's Inevitable Ups and Downs.*

Sequoia begins her work with me by having me take an assessment to find out what season of the year I am in. Not surprisingly, I am in the "Winter of my soul." I roll the idea around in my mind and it rings completely true: The Winter of my soul. How amazing it is to have the truth of this experience reflected back to me. When I look outside and see all the barren trees and the gray, overcast sky, it is as if I am looking at myself in a mirror.

Sequoia's requests of me are simple: 1) Find a comfortable spot in my house that I declare my safe haven; 2) Go to my safe haven whenever I need to and write in a journal; and 3) Take my cues from nature by going out for a walk every day and observing nature's processes.

The moment Sequoia mentions a safe haven, I know immediately where it will be. It will be my bed.

When I think of all the beds I have ever slept in, I am reminded of a poem by Raymond Carver "The Car." There was "the car with no heater or defroster," and the "car with a hole in its muffler," and the list goes on and on. I remember my beds in a similar way; there was the bed with the spring that dug right into my side and the bed that smelled like a wet cat. Fortunately, my current bed rivals a five-star hotel for luxury. It is a dark, rich, mahogany sleigh bed with curves that were almost unbearably inviting. And in an uncharacteristic splurge, I had bought the most luxurious pillows, sheets, and goose-down comforter I could find.

This is the bed of my dreams. And this is the bed I will allow myself the gift of staying in. Without Sequoia's help, I would never have given myself permission. I might have stayed in bed by default, too grief-stricken to get up, but I would not have enjoyed the experience. It would have been riddled with angst. I'd be tossing and turning and wracked with feelings of despair.

This will be different. I will honor my need to stay in bed. I will honor my need to stop and to mourn, and I will do it with full consciousness. I will lovingly wrap the comfort of this dream bed around me, and I will accept it with gratitude. Now that I have identified my safe haven, my mourning journey begins in earnest.

Chapter 6

✤

The Great Loneliness

I am in the deep heart of darkness, the archetypal dark night of the soul. Or as my mentor Sequoia is showing me—Winter. I have to face this, and I have to face it alone. I begin to develop a sense of relief that I don't have friends or family to comfort me. Or more precisely, to distract me because all the distractions in the world could not take away my sorrow. In Elizabeth Lesser's book, *Broken Open*, she talks about the wisdom of the Caribou Eskimos from northern Canada who understand that "true wisdom lives far from mankind, out in the great loneliness, and can be reached only through suffering."

I am flattened and immobilized. I imagine that if friends had been around they probably would have tried to coax me back into activities. They would want me to "snap out of it" and "get back to my old self." But I see the beauty in this state. And I am beginning to appreciate the wisdom in it as well. In my immobilized state, all my attachments to life are severed. Nothing calls to me. Nothing interests me. Nothing distracts me. Therefore, nothing prevents me from going where my soul naturally longs to go.

My soul longs to go down. In Thomas Moore's book, *Care of the Soul*, he explores the "gifts of depression." Moore uses Jungian psychology to explore the differences between our "anima" and our "animus." He calls our anima "wet" and describes it as "full of imagination, close to life, empathic, and connected to people" and our animus as "dry" and in need of "an excursion into the far-off regions of cold." Moore speaks well of depression as adding "ballast" to the soul, and bemoans that if we continue treating depression as an illness to be cured mechanically or chemically, then we may lose the gifts that only depression can provide.

I am going down, down, down. There is a physical pull on my body to stop, which is infinitely stronger than I am. No amount of personal willpower will allow me to override the force of this experience. My major coping skill—toughing it out—is useless here. There is only one thing I can do, and that is to surrender. Wait. That's not entirely true. There are other choices I could make, but they all entail numbing the pain and I'm not interested in any choice that involves avoiding this pain. I will travel into the "great loneliness" and endure my suffering without anesthesia.

In Eckhart Tolle's book, *A New Earth*, he writes about the extraordinary value of surrender. He says that "form means limitation," but we are here not just to experience limitation but to overcome limitations. He elaborates, "some limitations can be overcome on an external level" but there are others "that can only be overcome internally" through surrender. Tolle goes on to say, "The surrendered state of consciousness opens up the vertical dimension of depth. Something will then come forth from that dimension into this world, something of infinite value that would have remained unmanifested."

With weekly contact with Sequoia as my lifeline, I surrender to this call of my soul and down I go. On the dimension of form, I still vaguely recognize my surroundings. I can see that my body is lying on the bed but my soul is descending ever deeper. My sorrow seems to be a deep abyss with no bottom. I wonder how far I will go?

Chapter 7

❧

My Kindred Spirit

During my daily walks I devote myself completely to observing nature. What is She doing? The trees and the plants are all still. There is no outward growth. All the sap or life-force of the plant has gone into the roots. On one of my walks, I notice the starkness of a severely pruned rosebush. It has been reduced to a bare stump with only a few gnarled branches, and I recognize the rosebush as my kindred spirit. I can imagine the roses in full bloom and I remember when I had been in blossom too.

Memories of my life on the island of Kauai waft back to me like the fragrant trade winds that used to blow my sheer bedroom curtains into billowing sails. On Kauai everything seemed to be in bloom both within and without. I was greeted each morning by bright hibiscus flowers outside my kitchen window, exuberant chirping of birds, and the radiant glow of love on my true love's face. We had a charmed existence where everything seemed to come easily.

It was a perpetual Summer on the island and it was my internal Summer as well. Friends were in abundance and we all seemed to be on the same aloha wave-length. Now as I look back, it seems so very far away. Could I go back to Kauai and surround myself with my old friends? Could I, once again, rest in her gentle breezes? I know intuitively that I couldn't. I know that if I tried it would be disaster. The warmth and the sunshine would only serve to mock the coldness I feel inside.

It's so easy to love Summer because ease is one of Summer's primary characteristics. But Winter is tough. It requires some preparation and determination to get through. The more I surrender to it, the more I can see its properties. One thing I begin to appreciate is Winter's raw power. This power of the mourning process is working on me just the way the power of Winter is working on the outside world. Nothing escapes. Any idea I ever cherished of being a strong person becomes laughable. I am held tightly in the vise grip of nature's power. My personal willpower has been crushed and my identity has been shattered.

Again, I wonder how far down I will go as things continue to get darker and darker. There is literally nothing that has any power to uplift me as I surrender to the downward pull in my life. In the past I would have been afraid of never returning from such a sorrow, but this time I surrender to the descent because, in truth, I don't have the energy to resist it. Without all my panicked resistance to the darkness that envelopes me, an amazing thing happens—I feel safe.

As I accept the darkness, I suddenly feel held and nurtured. I am reminded of the poem "Footprints," where the soul in anguish cries out to God wondering where He was when she was so in need. God answers that He was carrying her.

Now I am being carried. The experience is reminiscent of what happened during Bob's memorial service when I was wailing out loud. I could actually feel the prayers buoying me up and carrying me through that painful passage. And now, I feel the all-encompassing power of God's love cradling me like an infant.

Chapter 8

❧

The Peace Which Passes all Understanding

A calm surrender envelopes me. I can rest in the darkness without a fear of the dark. I am developing what the Bible refers to as the "peace which passes all understanding." (Phil. 4:7) I could never have understood how I could lose my fear of the dark, of the unknown, of "the great loneliness" by going into the loneliness. It is the most unexpected gift of my life. It is the gift of true mourning. And this gift is given by grace and received by surrender. I don't have to work hard for it, or earn it, or deserve it. And most importantly, it isn't achieved through willpower.

The only thing I have done is determine that I won't run away from this mourning process. When everyone else is clamoring for me to come here or go there, or do this or don't do that, I keep my own counsel. As everyone shouts their own "bad advice," as Mary Oliver calls it in her poem "The Journey," I turn to my own voice. As I proceed deeper and deeper into this journey, the clearer my own voice becomes.

I am saving my life by losing my life. I lose everything I had known about myself. I lose all my interests, appetites, and desires. What a freedom I discover in this! It's as if everything I had known myself to be is wiped clean. I can start fresh. I can be reborn. And who do I want to be?

In the dark womb of my existence, I am starting the gestation process of my rebirth. As Carol McClelland writes in *Seasons of Change*, "If you want to make some long-lasting, significant changes in your life, you'll need to bite the bullet, fight your impulse to escape, fend off the criticism from inside and out, and consciously begin your journey into Winter."

I marvel at how easy it is to see all that is worth living for in the darkness of my mourning. I can understand how life is understood through contrasts. Anyone who has lost their health understands the deep longing for recovery and sees how priceless the gift of good health appears. In fact, doesn't the vantage point of being ill afford the best view of being well?

Likewise, to be without friends provides the best seat in the house to understand what friendship is all about. In the "great loneliness" I long, not only to have friends again, but to be a better friend. I long to be a friend who stays in touch on every level. On the physical level, I imagine how I will stroke my friends' arms, and hold their hands, and rub their shoulders, and pat them on the back. When I see them I will let my face light up with the full expression of my joy.

In my memory, I drift back to my life on Kauai. I had been working for a counseling agency that had let a corporate mentality inflict a chilling stranglehold on its policymakers. Everything was being reduced to numbers and success rates. When the heart went out of the agency, the inevitable manipulation of statistics became the overriding principle. It reminded me of Mark Twain's observation that there are "Lies, damn lies, and statistics." It was a huge struggle to keep my humanity in that humanity-squelching environment.

There was one native Hawaiian woman who worked for the agency who managed to do both—meet her quotas and keep her heart intact. She had a one-hundred percent success rate. I was naturally eager to learn her secrets. During a weekend training, I buddied up to her and asked her directly to share her insights with me. She told me to treat the clients "like family and forget the numbers." On our plane ride home we sat together. Without any self-consciousness, she stroked my arm and held my hand lovingly as we talked. As a North American woman, I had not been raised to hold my women friends' hands, and I couldn't help but notice my initial discomfort over her affectionate behavior. Fortunately, within a few moments, I was able to take to it like a cat takes to a bowl of milk. This beautiful woman was teaching me the natural way to treat another human being. What intimacy I've missed out on I thought to myself as I imagined a life where I too reached out and touched all those I loved.

If I ever emerge from this solitude, I determine that I will be a person who reaches out and makes the first move. I will extend my hand, along with my heart, and make the human connection that I value so deeply. This new sense of myself is being born in the dark womb of my dark night. It is light born of the darkness. It's all making perfect sense as I develop my new appreciation for the dark. After all, how can you even see light without the dark?

Chapter 9

Marching to the Drumbeat of My Grief

When March rolls around, I determine it will be a month that I dedicate to full-on grieving. I have heard of this idea in relationship to worry. The idea is to fully dedicate yourself to worry but do it for a prescribed time period, such as ten minutes. You worry, worry, worry for the allotted time and then when the ten minutes are up, you move on.

In March I grieve wholeheartedly. I cry as often and as deeply as I want. I do not watch television, or listen to the radio, or chat idly on the phone, or go out to movies, or do any one of the countless other things I might fill my days with. Instead, in March I grieve. This is it.

I silently march along to the drumbeat of my own grief. I see no one and I talk to no one with the exception of Sequoia (and my devoted son) on my weekly calls. I take walks in nature and observe. I stay in the safe haven of my bed and write in my journal or dive deeply into my sorrow. I limit my meals to two meals a day because I don't have the interest or energy to eat any more than that. In the afternoon, I work on photo albums. And then I cry. The days follow each other in close succession; each one a mirror image of the last.

In the past, being a good neighbor was a key source of my identity and something that I had prided myself on. Now, along with my identity, my pride vanishes too and I do something I have never done before. I totally disregard my neighbors. Every afternoon around two o'clock, I crank up my stereo as loud as it will go and blast the emotionally wrenching rock song "Reign Over Me" by the Who while I cry my heart out. This lasts about ten minutes. I then turn the stereo off and am done for the day. My neighbors never complain, either because they aren't home during the day, or because they recognize my temporary insanity for what it is.

On April 1st, I receive a phone call and the caller brings to my attention that it is April Fools day. I hear the word April with great astonishment. It's as though I suddenly feel an upwelling of energy lift me up and out of my darkness. It is April and I will be turning over a new calendar page. In the house, I have three calendars, one in the kitchen, one in the bedroom, and one in the office. As I go from room to room turning the pages, my body seems to surge with new feelings of life.

March is over. I have lived through the month that I dedicated to deep mourning. I have been true to my husband's memory, true to myself, and true to the season. But now it is April and life is suddenly filled with glimmers of possibilities. What will I do? I don't know exactly. All I know is that it is April and I have never noticed what a beautiful word this is. I think to myself that if I had a daughter I would like to name her April.

Chapter 10

Spring

Sequoia continues to coach me to take my cues from nature. I'll never forget the first time I see a yellow forsythia bush in all its true splendor. How extraordinary it looks! I won't have to figure this all out by myself; instead nature will be showing me the way. The life force that wells up in the forsythia is the same life force that is lifting me up. From the cold and gray of Winter comes the yellow of Spring.

What a revelation this is to me! I don't have to try to feel better or cheer up. All I have to do is observe and be open to the process. It's obvious that nature is coming back to life and so am I. When Winter is over, Spring will come of its own accord— naturally and effortlessly. As my energy returns, a wave of determination comes over me and I make an instantaneous decision: I will clear out Bob's clothes immediately.

I don't want to be one of those widows who keeps her deceased husband's clothes hanging lifelessly in the closet for years. I don't want to bury my face in his smell and wallow in the longing for what was. No. I will donate all his clothes as soon as possible. I will clean out our closet and let in the fresh air of Spring.

After being without any physical energy or enthusiasm for so long, this surge of life I feel coursing through my veins is exhilarating and takes me by surprise. Within an hour's time, I have all of Bob's clothes sorted and put into boxes. I vacuum the closet and rearrange my clothes to utilize the whole space. I know that it is good Feng-Shui to clean out that which you do not utilize, and I feel good when I see my newly functional closet.

When I look at all of Bob's clothes stacked in boxes in the hallway, however, my heart suddenly sinks with the same rapidity with which it rose. This is so final. How can I take these clothes away? It will be more than I can bear. Defeated and dejected again, I slink back into bed. In synchronicity with my internal experience, icy winds suddenly rattle the windows and the sky dramatically turns overcast and gray again. This time it feels colder in the cold and darker in the dark. But this is the way Spring is, isn't it? It doesn't come all at once.

Chapter 11

Not a Time of Reason

Within a day or two the phone rings. It's a friend from the retreat center where Bob and I had volunteered. She's driving up from Florida and can stop by my place if I need help with anything. Suddenly Carla doesn't sound like Carla anymore, she sounds like the voice of an angel. She is willing to drive out of her way to stop at my empty house in the middle of nowhere just to see if I need any help. It's unbelievable to me the timing of this visit, and I marvel at the grace of it all. It feels more like a divine intervention and I know that I have never needed a friend more in my whole life than I do in this moment.

When Carla arrives, I remain in awe. She jumps right into the task of taking Bob's things to the thrift store. In addition, she comes back with a stack of brochures about local services that she thinks might be of some benefit to me. She explains them all in great detail but I can't follow her or take in what she is saying. Despite the fact that I have never needed a friend more, or been more grateful for the timing of her visit, I find that I can't reciprocate. I can't follow the rattle of her conversation or be a gracious host. To my great dismay, I feel incapable of connecting with her at all. Wasn't I just dreaming of what a wonderful friend I would be if I were ever given the chance again?

It isn't long before I find her presence unbearably jarring. Eventually we have a little falling out about which route might be the best for her journey on. She seems to want to discuss an infinite number of options. As my patience wears thinner and thinner, I beg her to understand that I don't have the energy to care about which route she takes. Like a belligerent drunk who doesn't have exact recall of what he said or did after a drinking binge, I have only a vague memory of saying something to the effect of I didn't care how she got out—as long as she got out!

I'm pretty sure Carla never forgave me for my rudeness and I remain ashamed of the way I behaved as well. However, I do understand how jangled my nerves were and how much I was not in my "right" mind. This incident reminds me of something I had read about Native American belief systems around grieving. To the Native Americans it was considered wise to refrain from engaging a grieving person in conversation. It was understood that grieving requires energy and to engage someone in conversation was like taking precious energy from them. It was also understood that the grieving person had nothing to give at this time.

In my interaction with Carla she seemed to be operating from the assumption that she had gone out of her way to be a good friend to me and that I would reciprocate. It was a reasonable assumption. But grieving is not a time of reason. It is a time of intense emotions where emotions demand their due time. A neuroscientist would most likely explain it in terms of a shift from higher-level cognitive functions in the cerebral cortex to the primitive emotions of the limbic system: What could be called an emotional hijacking.

Whatever the specific explanation might be, I know that I could not focus my mind enough to follow her conversation. Even though I saw the paradox in the fact that I had been longing for friends, and pledging to be a better friend if I were ever given the chance again, I know that this is not the time for it. After Carla left, I am more grateful than ever to be left alone.

Chapter 12

A Call from the Universe

Midway through April, a knock comes at my door that I can't ignore. It seems to be life telling me it's time to pay attention to my surroundings again.

The knock actually comes in the form of a rock being thrown at my window! While sitting quietly at my computer, I am jarred back into reality by a loud crash that hits just inches from my face. My initial reaction is pure shock followed by outrage. Looking out the window, I can see the guilty party.

It is Malika, my eleven-year-old neighbor. Sometime before my husband died, Malika and her little brother

Washington had gotten locked out of the house. It turned out that their older sister, who was supposed to be watching them, had missed her bus home from school. I had invited the children in and given them the only kid-friendly items I could find: microwave popcorn and grape juice. This turned out to be a big hit, and if the children had it their way they would have been locked out every day. In addition to the snacks, I seemed to have given them some sorely needed attention while we drew pictures and colored together around my kitchen table.

During the Christmas holidays I had invited Malika and Washington to see the movie, "Charlotte's Web" and that seemed to seal the deal—they were permanently attached to me. Every time I saw them after that they jumped up and down and begged for popcorn, grape juice, and another trip to the movies. While the old adage "out-of-sight, out-of-mind" seemed to hold true for the Winter months, by April, Malika couldn't contain herself any longer and decided to get my attention one way or another.

As I walk from the office outside to the scene of the crime, I recognize this as both a call for help and a call from the Universe to start paying attention to my surroundings again. I breathe in and decide I will answer this call. What is life asking from me? I look at the window and, fortunately, it is only nicked. But the screen is torn. The damage doesn't seem to warrant any repair, but the act of throwing the rock does. Why does a little girl throw a rock directly at a window? And what will I do about it?

I weigh my options. If I take the girl home and report it to her mother, the girl will most likely get a spanking. I know that a violent act met with a violent act perpetuates the circle of violence but I want to respond without violence. I will express my disappointment with her behavior while keeping my heart open to her as a precious little child worthy of love. Simultaneously, I will give her consequences for her behavior. So I take Malika home and ask her mother if I can administer the consequences myself rather than having her spanked. Her mother looks quizzical but agrees.

I will put Malika to work in my garden and let her pull my weeds. She will need to pull one hundred weeds to pay for her wrongdoing. I solemnly give Malika gloves, a trowel, a glass of water, and some instructions. Then I sit back and count the weeds as she brings them to me. The first ten weeds are pulled with tears and anguish. I sit watching her work with calm approval and her tears quickly turn to a sense of industriousness and curiosity. Before she knows it, she is up to fifty and has the job half done.

By the time Malika reaches one hundred weeds she is all smiles. We are having a good time again. And that's what she wanted. Afterwards I invite her in to draw me another picture while I cook dinner. She jumps at the chance. When she finishes the picture she brings it over to me and my eyes well up with tears. Malika has painted a flower pot with five flowers in it. In each of the flowers she had written a word: "weeding—is—a—wonderful—job!"

Chapter 13

❧

Making Everything Beautiful

Now that I have opened the door to communication with the neighbor children again, they intensify their pleas to be taken to another movie. My query into whether or not they had any money for a movie is met with blank stares and the response that they "ain't got none." Hmmm. Maybe there is more I can do. I think about it and decide to hire them to help me pick up trash by the side of the road. I will pay them two dollars for filling up a trash bag. I arrange for them to help me on Saturday morning before it gets too hot, and then I will take them to the dollar movie theater at noon.

When they report for duty on Saturday morning they are less than enthusiastic. Nevertheless, I suit them up with gloves and reflecting vests, give them some cautionary instructions about watching out for broken glass and cars and sticking close to me, and off we go. Within minutes they are literally skipping and singing the praises of our efforts: "Look, Miss Elizabeth, we're making everything beautiful!" and "I love working!" and "Earning money is fun!"

In about forty-five minutes time we have transformed an intersection that had been a painful eyesore back to lovely countryside again. We haul off our three bags brimming with trash and return home where I proceed to pay them. To dramatize the interaction, I pay them in quarters. I ask the children to hold out their hands and methodically count out each one. Their eyes are as big as saucers as they eyeball their stacks of gleaming coins. At the movie theater the children pay for their tickets with their own quarters. I love watching new connections being made in their little children's minds.

What a marvelous way for me to re-enter life. I am caring for the neighborhood children as if I cared—which I do. I am caring for the environment as if I cared—which I do. I am beginning to understand that I can't change the whole world but I can take personal responsibility for my little portion of it.

Chapter 14

Sorting

As April unfurls itself and the flowers bloom, so do I. Every day my energy returns bit by bit, and I find myself up and out of bed again.

I sort through Bob's belongings with equanimity and find pleasure in taking care of things in a way that honors him. For example, our friend Yvonne had joined a volunteer organization that distributed eyeglasses throughout remote villages in South America. The donated eyeglasses were collected, cleaned, repaired, and labeled for their prescription strength. The villagers would receive an eye exam from an optometrist and then be fitted with a pair of the donated glasses. Yvonne found great satisfaction in the process of fitting the villagers with their new eyeglasses. She had stumbled into this new calling of hers in an unusual way. Yvonne had saved and planned for two years to take a luxury cruise with her new husband. After taking the cruise, however, she found herself oddly disgusted with the decadence of the cruise ship. To her surprise, she found the "good life" left her cold and she longed to travel with heart and purpose. Yvonne found it through the organization "Give the Gift of Sight."

When a loved one is dying, one's perspective of money becomes so altered. Toward the end of Bob's life I found that I couldn't give money any attention. Decisions were made that would never have been made before, and money slipped through our fingers like water. One of those financial decisions was to buy Bob two new pairs of eyeglasses. What would have been financially prudent— and spiritually bankrupt—would have been to say, "Bob's dying so we won't waste any money." Bob simultaneously experienced this shift in perspective about money. Before our mutual shift, Bob and I had shared a value system that valued being frugal and being generous equally. We oscillated freely between these poles and found as much enjoyment in refraining from spending money as we did in spending it.

It goes without saying, then, that anyone who is frugal with their money loves yard sales. And Bob and I were not exceptions to the rule. Over the years of being together we had come across some wonderful bargains in vacuum cleaners, and I loved watching Bob fix them up as good as new. At the same time, a really good quality vacuum cleaner is something I had always privately longed for, and this is one of those marital quirks that only someone married would know. Bob knew that the way to my heart would never have been diamonds, or fancy cars, or clothes, but, oh, for a really good quality vacuum cleaner how wistful I would become (can I help it if I love cleanliness?)

About two weeks before Bob died, I had heard him talking in the night. I stumbled out of bed to see if he needed anything and found him placing an order over the phone with his credit card. He was ordering a top-of-the-line vacuum cleaner with all the bells and whistles. The cleaner arrived within the week, and it was everything I could have dreamed of and more; it was as light as a feather but could "pick up a bowling ball," it propelled itself, it folded down absolutely flat to vacuum under beds and furniture, and it had a twenty-year guarantee. I was smitten. By the time the vacuum arrived Bob couldn't speak anymore, so he could never explain in words why he bought it but we both understood anyway.

The morning that I spend packing up hundreds of dollars worth of Bob's brand new eyeglasses is a good morning for me. It is a morning that I take care of something that needs to be done and I do it well. I make the loving choice for Bob, and for me, and for Yvonne, and the Gift of Sight organization, and for an unknown villager somewhere. I am simultaneously sorting out my belongings as well as my priorities.

Chapter 15

The Doors of Possibility

To feel up again, after being so down for so long, feels a bit intoxicating. I can live and I will live—and I will love! I love the gruff man at the post office, the bookish librarian, the baby cooing in the stroller, the flowers, the trees, the birds and the bees. I feel as though the song lyrics, "Oh What a Beautiful Morning!" were written just for me. Rather than focusing my love so intently on just one person I see that I can spread my love out to the entire world.

In this expansive mood I begin feeling very international again. I'm a citizen of the world who is in love with the world. This gives me the idea to check into teaching

English overseas again. Yes. That's it! I'll go to Europe, I think to myself. That's the Hollywood tradition that I've been steeped in, too. After the heroine loses her husband, she promptly boards a cruise ship to France. Why didn't I think of this sooner? It's perfect. I'll immerse myself in Renaissance art, and take photographs of enchanting chalets in the French countryside as I lick my wounds. I'm becoming a new person so it's only fitting that I become reborn into a new culture.

After perusing job openings on a website for teaching English abroad I find an opening that sends me to the moon. My hairs are standing on end and I'm tingling from head to toe. There is a one-month position in Paris teaching English through the arts at a summer art camp for international students. I am energized by the possibility and can feel myself waking from this dark night into full-throttle living. I write a cover letter with a proposal that I teach a month-long course in the art of video production; including writing a script, shooting the video, and editing and post-production. Within the day I have emailed my proposal, resume, and references from Huangshan University where I taught English in China.

The doors of possibility have swung open and I'm amazed and dazzled. I could never have conceived of such a wonderful opportunity just one month ago. How marvelous and incredible this world is! Bob would love this for me, too. He would want me to continue on to Paris like we had planned for our tenth anniversary of being together. I would see the Eiffel tower for both of us, and when I rode the elevator to the top he will be right there with me.

For the next few days after submitting my application, I live as though I have the job and my worldview changes dramatically. I am no longer a lonely person stuck in the middle of nowhere. The excitement of my upcoming adventure propels me forward and I continue to settle Bob's affairs with alacrity. The feeling of being stuck in molasses is long gone.

The response I had been waiting for arrives in an email. I am hired! You can imagine my elation. This time I even impressed myself. What a rebound! The pay is fantastic, which it needs to be to cover the plane tickets and housing. The school will assist the teacher in finding off-campus housing within walking distance. There will be a lot to do to prepare an interesting curriculum and lesson plans for a one-month program. It will take a lot of prep work and packing but it will be worth it. This will be an opportunity of a lifetime and I will rise to the challenge and embrace it.

I feel like a basketball that had been held under the water. I am popping up and out of the grief that had held me in a vise grip. When I tell my various friends and family, they are equally impressed. The simple idea of the way life can change on a dime is uplifting. Each day brings unlimited potential if we are only open-minded enough to imagine it. What will happen next? I wonder. Who will I meet in Paris? Where will my life take me? Where am I willing to let my life take me?

For about a week I live in the euphoria of unlimited access to my dreams. I can manifest the life that I am courageous enough to create. It is exhilarating and all is right with the world. As I delve into the details of my new employment offer, I understand that I will have to put down a deposit for my housing as well as pay for my plane tickets. Yes, that is reasonable; I would need housing so, of course, I would have to secure it. Nothing unreasonable about that … or was there?

I'd never seen this school or met the individuals who run it, or seen the housing. Yes, they had a website, and the job offer seemed bona-fide, and the email communications all appeared to be on the up and up. There was nothing to provoke suspicion of any kind. But how would I know? Today countless interactions are conducted via the Internet. This is the modern age. In the past I had obtained employment in China through a similar process. But what if? What if this were a scam? What a horrifying thought. What if this were a scam that operated on people's fantasies? There must be a way to verify the organization's legitimacy.

I suddenly remember that a friend of a friend lives just outside of Paris and I decide to contact him. He writes back with an extreme cautionary warning. He has never heard of anything positive coming out of these language schools and he could not confirm the existence of this school.

When I send another email to the school expressing my concerns, the whole interaction collapses like a puff of smoke. I shudder at the thought of charging off to Paris on a pipe dream. I would have squandered an incredible amount of time, energy, and precious financial resources only to find myself lost, and alone, and unloved in the city of love.

What a cruel hoax. And how foolish I felt.

On my weekly coaching call with Sequoia I confess the whole fiasco with my tail between my legs, feeling thoroughly deflated. She reframes the incident in the loving light of the Seasons of Change work. After such a long cold Winter, having bursts of energy is euphoric. But this is Spring. She redirected me to really study the nature of Spring. One day it is bright and sunny with glorious life bursting forth into radiant blossoms and the next day it is cold, and wet, and rainy, and gray again.

Sequoia explained that "charging ahead" without well-thought-out plans is one of the common pitfalls we face in the Springtime of our lives. We examine the alternative of selecting our seeds carefully and planting and tending them slowly. I can manifest my dreams but I need to work in harmony with the nature of life. What a comforting realization.

Chapter 16

Where there is Injury, Pardon

Toward the end of April I am still "experiencing Spring storms" and "struggling with re-entry." I'm not in bed, however, and I'm not in tears all the time, which I am grateful for. I'm not exactly jumping for joy, but a calm acceptance of my lack of joy has a certain pleasure in it.

Somewhere along the way, my voice has changed and is discernibly lower—even raspy. I remember years ago trying to imitate the sexy voice of a certain radio announcer, Dahlila, from the smooth jazz station in L.A. with absolutely no success at all. But now I am speaking with a voice that seems to originate from my bowels. My parents, whom I had been functionally estranged from for many years, were moved to come and visit. They want to stay three days. I know that I am not yet up to company but these are my parents and I accept the gift of their intention. I won't try to put on a happy face or entertain them. Instead I will allow them to share in my mourning. It is clear that Bob's death had affected them deeply, and they share as much. They say that they have taken the opportunity to make their own burial arrangements.

Another of the unexpected gifts of Bob's passing is in my parent's response. With a newly awakened sense of their own mortality, they are on their very best behavior. They don't complain, criticize, pick fights, or go on soap-boxes about their views of right and wrong. In fact, for once in our mutual lives, we don't seem to need to be in the strait-jacket of our roles as parent or child. For three beautiful days we are just human beings being human together. We get along so well and it is so pleasant to have their company that I scratch my head as to what we ever fought about in the first place. After all, we aren't so different.

The day before they are leaving, my mother brings up an old resentment. She asks if I remember asking her why I should listen to her because she had never "done anything of any value; never written a book, or painted a picture, or had a career." Did I remember telling her that I thought that she was "nothing and a big, fat, nobody?"

Did these words come out of my fourteen-year-old mouth? Where are words stored? I wonder. And memories? Such old memories, are they still there? As my mother speaks these words, words that seemed to be buried in the deepest part of her being, words that seemed to be the impetus and fuel behind her actions and non-actions towards me, I feel them in my body. My cruel words and sharp tongue seem to fit me like a glove.

It is similar to seeing the unique thumbprint that allows high-security access to secret places in action-adventure movies. I have to claim ownership of these words because there is a lasting memory imprint in my body that I can't deny. How ironic. The mother that I have always perceived as being unkind, I can now see was simply wounded by my unkindness. Oh, we reap what we sow, don't we? Perhaps it's true that I was the child and she was the adult and she should have been evolved enough not to respond like a child herself. But who's to say? And will I continue passing judgment indefinitely?

Judgment. This is another family—as well as cultural—legacy I recognize. In the darkness, I get to decide if I will carry this trait forward. Will I drag it along with me into my new life? Or will I put it down? Will I "lay my burdens down" as the gospel songs implore? Or will I pick them back up and carry them forward? What a gift this total shattering of identity is. It has broken me open and now I am free to sort through the rubble of my being and carry with me only what I consciously choose to pick up.

As Saint Francis of Assisi taught us, isn't it better to understand than to be understood? Where there is hatred, can I sow love? Where there is injury, pardon? Isn't it in pardoning, that we are pardoned? I recognize this as a holy moment and I drop to my knees and ask my mother's forgiveness. After profusely apologizing, I seek to shine the light of understanding on the situation. Yes, I was wrong to say such hurtful things and I willingly admit this.

Without negating my responsibility, I ask my mother to consider the possibility that at age fourteen maybe I wasn't coming up with original thinking but simply spouting the sexist stereotypes that I was being exposed to? Perhaps it was society that devalued women and saw the role of mother as "nothing." I told her that I've come to disagree completely with that viewpoint and assure her that there isn't anything I value more than the sacred feminine.

During a tour of the house the first day my parents arrived, I had spent a long time talking about a picture that hung on my bedroom wall. The picture was one of an old-fashioned woman in a farmhouse with a sleeping baby on her lap. She was gazing at the baby adoringly, along with a three or four year old daughter. The caption of the picture was "Sweet Dreams." I'd explained how much I love and cherish that painting and how much comfort it brings me to look at it every day. I believed the picture was given to me by God to bring Bob and me solace during our trying times. This was the first picture I'd bought for this new house, and it transformed the bare white walls.

As I continue speaking to my mother, I tell her that if she wants to know how I really feel about mothers and a mother's love, then she should remember how much I love the painting on my bedroom wall. I probably value a motherly love above all things. As I said these words, my mother sobbed with the intensity of the Old Faithful geyser. Her body shakes and she gasps for air as she cries and cries for a good ten minutes. Eventually, her tears subside and she calms down again.

The next day as my parents are preparing to leave, I notice the date is May 1st. It will be Mother's Day in a couple weeks. Instead of sending my mother a card through the mail, I decide to give her a gift in person. I ask her to sit down a minute and wait. I go into the bedroom, take the picture of the old-fashioned mother off the wall, and wrap a ribbon around it. When I present her with the picture she says that she can't take it because it means so much to me. I tell her that's exactly why I want her to take it. My mother cries again.

Chapter 17

A Bubbling Spring

In May, I receive an unusual request from my neighbor. Her six-year-old son has been expelled from the school bus through the end of the year, and she wants to know if I will drive Washington to school in the mornings and pick him up in the afternoon. Good God what a request, I think. It isn't just one day—it is until the end of the school year, which would be another six weeks! "Isn't there another child who goes to school that Washington could ride along with?" I ask. "No, they all take the school bus." What a dilemma. This is seriously inconvenient for sure. But if there's one thing I've learned about life it's this:

What I think is happening and what is really happening are usually two very different things.

I know that I will have to say "Yes." Apparently the Universe wants me to spend some time with Washington. I've had an inkling that I needed to spend time with this six-year-old neighbor right from the start. Since my husband was older, I knew going into the relationship that I would probably lose him one day. I thought to myself that when that happened, I would refuse to shrink into bitterness, or self-pity, but instead would look around me and find a child who needed love. Wherever I ended up in life, I knew there would be a child who would need me. And I would need that child to help me reconnect to life. The moment I laid eyes on Washington, I knew without the slightest doubt that he was the one.

Even though I had this knowing, I didn't actively pursue it. But when the Universe steps in to make the time for us, I surrender to the inevitable. Picking him up in the morning is an exercise in adorability because he is such a bundle of enthusiastic energy. Trying to calm him down enough to fasten his seat belt is like trying to capture a butterfly. It is the afternoon that sorely tries my patience. I have to get in the queue of cars and inch forward for twenty minutes before I see his smiling face. And then everything made sense. It isn't long before I understand our deeper level of connection. Washington lost his own father to cancer just a year ago. On the car rides home he needs to talk about his Daddy. Oh sweet boy how I understand your sorrow. You can talk to me and I will listen.

Simultaneously, Washington is all about life. He is a bubbling spring so close to the Source of Life. So pure. So fresh. So unspoiled. One of Washington's favorite things to do is D-A-N-C-E. That boy is full of razzmatazz. Completely free of any self-consciousness Washington takes every opportunity to bust a move. He is wired that way, as if his little ears are always perked up and on the alert for any sound of music. And when he hears it, he feels it. And when he feels it, he dances it. The boy is a natural.

When my stepdaughter Sarah delights me by sending a singing card for Mother's Day, I only have to open the card and Washington instantaneously dances. It doesn't matter what he's doing or where he is, if he hears music—he dances! I play up this effect by opening and closing the card randomly, and each time it tickles my funny bone because he's like a puppet on a string. He can't keep himself from dancing.

During this time there's a popular television show that featured celebrities dancing in various styles, such as Tango, Salsa, and Ballroom. For fun I play my own home version of "Dancing with the Stars" with Washington by calling out the different genres. He can transition from ballet, pirouetting through my living room, to hip-hop without missing a beat. Watching Washington make these seamless transitions from one dance to the next helps me get a perspective on the grand dance of our lives. We can dance one discrete style at one moment in time, but the dance keeps on.

Spending time with Washington is like plugging into a Life-Source living socket. And he likes spending time with me, too. Is it because I need him? Aren't we all looking for a place to belong? Or that I can accommodate both his sorrow and his joy? They are both so real. One is not more important than the other.

Or is it that I want to see him dance? I am the appreciative audience, and maybe what the dancer needs more than anything is someone who wants to watch him dance. Often, Washington starts to tell me something and is too excited to slow down enough to actually spit it out. He becomes all breathless and stammers, "Miss Elizabeth." Yes, I say. "Miss Elizabeth." Yes, I say again. "Ummm, oh, ummm, do you want to see me dance?" There's nothing in this world I like better, I think to myself as I say: Yes. Yes I do!

Chapter 18

What is Ready to be Born

By the middle of May I've sorted through all of Bob's stuff and taken care of the seemingly endless mountain of paperwork. My twelve weeks of Seasons of Change coaching has ended and now all that's left is me. I've come through the dark of Winter and I've experienced the burst of energy that accompanies Spring, along with the Spring storms. Now it's time for me to make a move.

In Ted Loder's exquisite book of prayers, *Guerrillas of Grace*, he writes, "In this season of short days and long nights, of grey and white and cold, teach me the lessons of endings: children growing, friends leaving, jobs concluding, stages finishing, grieving over, grudges over, blaming over, excuses over." He goes on to say, "teach me the lessons of beginnings: that such waitings and endings, may be a starting place..."

So I know it's time for a new starting place. But where? My son has been clamoring for me to move back to San Diego to live near him. My sister and nieces live in Chicago. My parents are aging in Florida. All of Bob's children and grandchildren live in California. The intentional community that I used to live in is beckoning me to return. Or the holistic retreat center where I was working when Bob became ill. I know my heart still belongs to Kauai, but somehow all the obvious choices hold no appeal to me. Every choice feels like I'm trying to go backwards in life.

I just don't know where to go, or what to do, and that's when a crushing stagnation set in. I'm now rattling around the empty house with my new-found energy bouncing off the walls. The house that has been my safe haven begins to feel like a prison. And you know what they say about "idle hands" being the "devil's workshop"? It doesn't take me long to get myself in trouble with the Internet again. This time I see a commercial for a "Free Personality Profile" on the mega-dating site, e-Harmony.

Bored, stuck in the middle of nowhere, left to my own devices, and a sucker for Free Personality Profiles, I succumb to the Internet's lure for a second time. I sign on and answer an endless number of questions, stopping just short of actually joining. I want their freebie offer but manage to resist their persistent requests for membership. I print out my profile and find out that I'm an "Idealist" who many people mistake as being "too good to be true." I am reminded of Kermit the Frog's song, "It's Not Easy Being Green."

Later that evening when I check my email I'm stunned to find out that I have seven matches from e-Harmony. It seems that Tom, Dick, and Harry are all eager to meet me. I somehow feel like I've won the lottery and I discover that e-Harmony allows me to read these eager gentlemen's profiles all without joining. At first I'm like a kid in a candy store reading about all these tantalizingly available men until I read the line, "I like to be good to my subordinates."

Subordinates? Upon closer inspection I discover that this man is a local police chief. Something tells me that this would not be a match made in heaven no matter how honey-sounding the voice of e-Harmony's founder is. I manage to laugh this episode off and be done with it.

A few weeks later, however, I'm entertaining a girlfriend with this story and she convinces me to try Internet dating again, but this time I need to pick my site carefully. She swears by a site that caters to spiritual singles, and like a pair of teenage girls she coaxes me into trying it, too. All of her arguments sound so reasonable: 1) We need to set our intentions in life to get the results we want; 2) This is a new era of dating and this is how it is done; 3) You can be very selective and screen your potential dates carefully; and 4) You can cast a wider net than by just waiting to bump into Mr. Right at the local hardware store.

I decide to try this new site and approach it with the utmost of sincerity. I carefully write my profile and decide to pay for the service and join it upfront rather than just peeking. Everything is feeling very good when a man responds to my profile. Somehow this site knows who is online at any given time and members can alert other members if they are interested.

When I check out the man who is interested in me, I immediately become wildly infatuated. He is from the Big Island of Hawaii and his name is Palea. I sound out the name just like the character from West Side Story who sings about Maria. Pa-leee-aaah. And "suddenly I've found" music all around. "Say it loud and there's music playing. Say it soft and it's almost like praying."

I write an email to my friend who introduced the whole idea to me with the subject line: "I've just met a boy named Palea..." Afterwards we talk and it turns out she's interested in him too. Now we are just like teenagers and I use the immature line that "I saw him first!" Begrudgingly she "lets" me have him and I waste no time in contacting him. Why play hard-to-get at this stage of the game? I think to myself as I pour my heart out to the poor unwitting fellow.

The next morning I wake up buzzing from head-to-toe and turn on the computer eager for his response. Instead I find a gaping hole of nothingness and I begin a rapid plunge into despair. Fortunately, I see the emotional roller coaster that I'm riding and decide to slam on the brakes right then and there. What am I doing? I'm sitting in front of an inanimate box responding as if something real were going on. It's not unlike a movie where we scream as the bad guys jump out of the bushes and swoon as the lovers kiss, but it's nothing but a play of shadows and light.

I recognize that I've done it again. I've allowed myself to get swept up in a fantasy and I decide once again that I will pull the plug on this kind of behavior. For all I know this dreamy Palea from Hawaii could be a product of the website's creator, designed specifically to ignite the fires of lonely widows everywhere. And speaking of fraudulent, when I reread my profile—that I painstakingly crafted for hours—I see it is such a flattering portrait that it is closer to fiction than reality. Perhaps this is the woman I long to be.

Rather than sit and stew over this latest Internet fiasco, I decide that I will push myself away from the computer. I will embrace this day for what it is. I will walk my own journey through life and I will do it one day, and one step, at a time. I go outside in the fresh air and take a hike. Within minutes I come across a bushy-tailed red fox. When I see this fox I understand that this is a good omen for me. I am walking my own journey and I will be met with beauty along the way. I feel empowered.

When I return home I feel alive. I know I'm on the right track and I am prepared to face life head on. I erase my overly flattering profile and cancel my membership to the spiritual singles site. I acknowledge squarely that I'm not ready for dating, and I return to my process of mourning and coming out of mourning. I will not date for at least one year. I started this journey and I will see it through. I also give my notice that I will be moving. It's time for me to get out of this house.

Chapter 19

Breaking out of the Shell

I now have a "For Sale" sign in the front yard and I feel like a chick that has to break out of her shell. As I look at the sign that seals my fate, I know that I still don't know where I'm going. I realize that this is not the route most people take but I know enough about myself to know that if I don't force my decision-making process I could stay here stuck in limbo for all eternity. I prefer the discomfort of the unknown to the stagnation I feel in this house.

As I assess where I am in North Carolina I discover a buried yearning to live in the Blue Ridge Mountains. Right now I'm about five hours away and this would be a workable choice. I'm noticing that I have a new maturity about decision-making as I understand that this decision doesn't have to be the be-all and end-all decision. I just have to decide something and if the decision doesn't yield the results I want then I will course-correct and make another decision.

I had come across this idea years ago presented by Stephen Covey, the author of *Seven Habits of Highly Effective People*. He described how an airplane that is flying on autopilot is actually flying off-course ninety-five percent of the time, and the plane's internal programming is one that uses continual course-corrections to get the plane to its destination. He encourages us to use the same process in our own lives: Stop and check to see if we are "where we want to be" and if not, then course-correct. When I had initially read that advice I liked it but never fully applied it to my life. Now I will.

I decide to move to the Asheville area and begin researching my options. I contact a real estate agent friend who advises me to check out the outlying communities that circle Asheville for greater affordability and a more rural feel. As I explore the various towns that are an option for me I find one town that I am immediately and powerfully drawn to. The town has commissioned local artists to create sculptures of bears for its downtown area. These bears are part of a campaign to attract more tourists to visit with their campaign "Bearfootin' in Hendersonville."

I understand that the bear speaks to me because my animal totem is a bear. In the Native American tradition all people have an animal spirit that guides and instructs them. I have a picture of a bear that I have downloaded from the Internet on my bulletin bear with this inscription: "The power of the Bear totem is the power of introspection. The answers to all our questions lie within us. Each of us has the capacity to quiet our mind and know."

It goes on to say, "When you have a Bear totem, you are being guided to a leadership role. You must be fearless in defending your beliefs."(www.linsdomain.com) Despite the fact that I've often felt more like the cowardly lion from the Wizard of Oz than a great and mighty bear, I resonate to the truth of this guiding Spirit. I even had the blessing of meeting a bear face-to-face while taking a morning walk around a reservoir one time. When I stumbled upon the bear I understood it to be a gift. I looked into the bear's eyes as if I were looking into who I was destined to become.

I acknowledge that my decision-making process is not being governed by conventional thinking. Who moves to a town because they are called by their inner animal spirit? But I have started this journey and there is no turning back now. I am venturing deeper and deeper into my own knowing, and I will continue on. I didn't know how I would traverse this mourning journey; all I knew was that I would.

Now I realize that equally as important as diving into the mourning is coming out of it. But who will be there to help me? I will have to learn to rely solely on my "Internal Guidance System." I'm borrowing the phrase "Internal Guidance System" from Linda Joy Montgomery, a woman who lost her eyesight at age forty and went on to say that this was the best thing that had ever happened to her. She rejoiced in the opportunity to develop her inner-sight and to rely completely on her inner knowing. She even went to elementary schools and gave talks to the children on this topic.

I am breaking away from the stranglehold of societal expectations. My young nieces in Chicago have predicted that I will immediately return to California to live near my son. While it sounds reasonable, I know that I have no desire to live on the freeways of Southern California while I'm stuck in traffic or to hang onto my son's coat-tails. I will use my powers of introspection and I will chart my own course. All I have to do is learn to love what I love. The thirteenth-century poet, Rumi wrote: "When you do something from your Soul, you feel a river moving in you, a joy."

Chapter 20

Just what the Doctor Ordered

When I make the decision to move to Hendersonville everything falls into place easily. I follow my intuition to put my things into storage and just rent a room to get acquainted with the area. I find a local listing of shared housing options and immediately respond to one listing; a "cozy three bedroom home with large yard, porch, in-room Internet connection and private bath." When I call about the place, I am enchanted by the young woman, Grace, who answers the phone.

Grace and Stewart are newlyweds who are both going to graduate school. They are also fitness enthusiasts. Grace sends me pictures of them on top of various mountains. They are brimming with youthful vitality and I make all the arrangements to move in with them. On my moving day, July 1st, they happen to be out of town for the July 4th holiday. I hire a neighbor to help me drive a U-Haul truck and I'm full of curiosity as we approach the house. We drive through a charming neighborhood and end up on a picturesque, tree-lined street. The home is warm and welcoming and I breathe a sigh of relief as I enter the house in person.

On July 5th, the young couple returns from their trip to Michigan. They've driven all night long and look a bit bedraggled. We greet each other and I immediately like them both very much. Since I know they are tired, I keep our chatting to a minimum and go out to run errands. When I come back I see that the grass has been mowed. I mention that I'm surprised that they would have enough energy to mow the lawn after such a long drive. Grace tells me that Stewart can't wait to mow the lawn. She teases that he practically sits and waits for it to grow.

This is when it dawns on me how right this move is. This young couple, in their early twenties, is just what the doctor ordered for me. They are brimming with life. It's as though they are children playing at being adults and having a grand time of it. I try to remember back to a time when grocery shopping, or cooking dinner, or mowing the lawn, was fun, and I can but the memories are rusty. I'm grateful to have these two to remind me.

I feel like a kindly grandmother who finds everything they do simply adorable. For example, they have a certain television show that they are crazy about. They talk about it all week and on the night of the show they make it a grand production with a countdown of one-half hour to the show, ten minutes to start time, one minute and so on. They make cookies and popcorn and are glued to the set. They invite me to join them and while I have no interest in the particular show, I can't help but delight in watching them enjoy life so much. While they watch the television, I surreptitiously watch them.

Grace and Stewart's *joie de vivre* is contagious. The way they view the world as their playground full of fun and possibility is enlivening me and I too am filled with an adventurous spirit. I quickly find a local Unity church that is the hub of the community. Through this base every door seems to open to me. On just my second visit to the church I'm invited to join a group of folks for lunch afterwards, and I eagerly accept the invitation.

During the lunch I find myself sitting next to a beautiful woman, Joy, who is also new. She tells me a wonderful story about how she is living her dream. She's been a biology teacher in Florida her entire adult life. For the last ten years as her parents have aged, she's cared for them through various stages of Alzheimer's and dementia. It's been a long and difficult journey but they've left her with enough money to move to North Carolina and build her dream home in the mountains.

Joy goes on to say that all her wishes have come true except for one: She was able to build her dream home, have a loyal and wonderful neighbor, and now all she needs is a friend. My ears perk up and if it was possible to jump up and down in the seat I'm sure I do that too. At this moment, I couldn't help but think of Shakespeare's memorable line that "All the world's a stage and we are merely actors upon it." This is my cue and what music it is to my ears. "I'll be your friend!" I practically sing out.

This is the beginning of a friendship made in heaven. When I tell her my story she can't believe how synchronistic it is that we've both moved to Hendersonville without knowing anyone, and we've both only been here for less than a month. Joy tells me she had even gone so far as to tell a neighbor that she couldn't join her at her church today because she was "going to meet a friend" at the Unity church. Since she didn't really know anyone, this was a fib on one level, but on a deeper level it was a deep soul-yearning that she had expressed, and now it was coming true. From this point on we are like two peas-in-a-pod.

As I get to know my young homeowners' story better, I begin to understand why I've been led to move here. It turns out that Stewart had lost his mother at age fourteen. She had been a single parent and had been ill for some time before she died and Stewart was extremely devoted to her. He was left the house and the court ordered that his father live in the house with Stewart until he reached the age of eighteen. Apparently the father was a ne'er do well, and as soon as Stewart turned eighteen, he evicted him.

The problem is that Stewart never had anyone to guide him in his grief. His attachment to his mother exerted a crippling influence over his home. Grace confided in me that for years Stewart refused to let anyone touch any of his mother's belongings. When she died she had a cup of tea on her bedside table that Stewart could not bear to move for more than two years. Any attempt on Grace's part to decorate or renovate the home was met with irrational resistance on Stewart's part. He felt that to touch any of her belongings was somehow to desecrate her memory. I was able to demonstrate to Stewart that there are healthy and proactive ways to memorialize someone. I showed him how I had taken my wedding ring and had it welded together with Bob's. Whenever I wanted I could go to my jewelry box and take out our ring and put it on and wrap myself in the warm embrace of our happy memories.

We discussed which items in the house represented positive memories for him and which ones carried associations with illness and pain. We brainstormed ideas together about how he could joyously celebrate his mother's memory. It was as though Stewart's mother was speaking through me and saying, "Remember how much I loved you but it's time to leave the rest behind."

Chapter 21

Home at Last

In August I'm eating lunch at a local food co-op and I notice a newspaper lying open on the table. There is a home for sale that catches my eye. It's advertised as being a "quality remodel" with everything new—including the kitchen sink. The price is staggeringly low and I am bitten with curiosity. After living in both California and Hawaii where fixer-uppers are all in the million dollar range, this home seems like it's available for pocket change.

I call the number in the ad and reach a man who tells me his story. He got divorced a couple of years ago and stumbled upon this "fixer-upper." After two years of doing weekend renovations he ended up marrying a woman who owned a home closer to his work and they've decided to live there. He has never lived in the house and has no need for it but he did find the renovation process to be very therapeutic.

When I go to see the house, the outside is not much to look at. But the location is country living at its best. I arrive early and walk around getting a feel for the area. I picture myself being happy here. When I enter the house it's like a dream come true. Every square inch of the home has been renovated. It's a shining jewel on the inside and I can't believe my eyes. As we finish the tour and he leads me into the last room of the house I literally jump up and down, shouting, "I'll take it!"

I laugh to myself and with the seller as I realize that I've blown my bargaining advantage with my over-the-top enthusiasm for the place but I can't help it. Besides, I don't want to barter for this house. It's perfect in every way and I feel delighted to pay whatever the asking price is. In truth, I would have liked to pay much more, and I marvel at my good fortune at getting it for such a good deal. This is one of those joyous decisions in my life that requires no deliberation. It is an absolute resounding, "Yes!" This is my house and I know it.

Chapter 22

❦

Settling In

Waking up in my new home is a source of deep satisfaction for me. I recognize it as an opportunity for me to develop new healthy habits as well. I'll be turning fifty in October and I know I want to begin a practice of sustainable habits that will, God willing, serve me well into my old age. For example, I want to eliminate the habit of starting my morning with any caffeine. Even though I replaced coffee with green tea years ago, I feel it is still over-stimulating my nervous system and isn't truly in tune with my body.

For the first time in memory, I try waking up naturally. This takes some undoing of my habitual patterns. I used to revel in getting up and getting busy. I was my own little drill sergeant, and like the military I prided myself in getting more done "before nine a.m. than most people do all day." Now I allow myself to wake up naturally. I find myself stretching like a contented cat and often stay in bed for hours reading.

Eventually I get hungry or thirsty, and by that time I can roll out of bed on my own steam. I begin loving the feeling of waking up gradually. I love the way my energy increases in steady increments until I am going full-tilt. I marvel at recovering this most natural of human processes—generating my own energy.

I'm living my own ideal of voluntary simplicity and my sweet home is a source of great comfort for me. I lovingly tend to every chore. Whether I'm washing a pot, or watering my garden, I do it with full mindfulness. There are times when I just stop and notice something of beauty like the sunlight catching a drop of dew in the morning. Outside my bedroom window there is a honeysuckle bush with the most heavenly fragrance. I take the time to breathe it in.

The intentions that I put into my home yield palpable results. Everyone who comes over soon comments on how tranquil and soothing it is. The most compelling of these compliments come from the husband of one of my new friends. Sam is legally blind, and when he enters my home he says that it feels just like a sanctuary. Without being able to see anything, he senses the sacred atmosphere.

I'm creating my new life with each choice I make. I buy an old-fashioned push mower reveling in its low-carbon footprint and its nostalgic clickety-clack sound. I believe in living green and now I have an opportunity to express this more fully. As I plant seeds in the ground, I also know I am planting the seeds of my new self.

Just as I'm settling into my new surroundings—and into myself—I'm given an unexpected medical diagnosis. It's one of those diseases with an unpronounceable name a mile long. In essence, I have a small, and thankfully benign, lump on my auditory canal nerve pathway. I am told I have three options for treatment: I can either have a risky brain surgery to remove it, undergo chemotherapy, or have physical therapy. The brain surgery and chemotherapy options hold about as much appeal as … well … brain surgery and chemotherapy.

The physical therapy option suddenly holds great appeal. It turns out that I can grow new neural networks around the problem area but the only way for me to grow these new neural networks will be to exercise and push myself out of my comfort zone past any tendency I have to get dizzy. I marvel at the miracle of this crisis, remembering that within the Chinese characters representing crisis, one finds both danger and opportunity. I can do nothing and continue to struggle with balance issues or I can exercise and grow new neural networks right around my problem.

This seems to be a poetic metaphor for me and for us all. Like most Americans who know that they "should" exercise but are not particularly thrilled by the prospect, I've struggled in vain with my nagging sense of obligation to do it. However, life is now upping the ante. I am being given a chance to learn how to exercise in a way that will literally be lifesaving, and I'm struck by the irony of this dilemma.

I always love the way I feel after exercise. I love its stress-relieving qualities. In fact, I had even gone so far as to become certified as a personal trainer. Shortly after marrying Bob, I was so eager for him to maintain his health that I took a course through the International Sports Science Association in Exercise Science. Even though I felt completely out of my comfort zone, I trained with a two-time winner of the Mr. Universe title. I remember what a frumpy housewife I felt like at the time and how awkward it was for me to even be in a gym, much less getting certification as a trainer. Some internal prompting kept me going, however, and so like Gloria Steinem infiltrating the Playboy Bunny club, I continued on. I remember feeling privately appalled at a lot of what I was observing. Our teacher regaled us with stories of steroid abuse in the early days of Muscle Beach in California. He told us that he had personally seen a man pull his arms out of their sockets while trying to lift a weight that was significantly too heavy. While he told these stories as amusing anecdotes, I took careful mental notes as if I were an anthropologist studying a fascinating new tribe.

In fact, the tribe of self-proclaimed "gym rats" was a fascinating source of study. Since I had already been trained as a psychologist I couldn't help but notice all the psychologically unhealthy practices that were commonplace in the modern "health club." For example, the use of humiliating fat calipers to measure a person's percentage of body fat struck me as nothing short of barbaric.

The most glaring thing I noticed about the exercise industry is that the vast majority of personal trainers were all natural exercise enthusiasts. Now, this makes sense that the field of exercise would be inhabited by those who find a natural affinity for exercise. However, I was starting to notice the limitation of this natural selection process. In Howard Gardner's illuminating study of multiple intelligences, he identifies physical intelligence as an innate gift. The problem as I could see it was that those with a natural proclivity to exercise often have little empathy for those with other gifts, such as musical intelligence, social intelligence, or us verbal types.

Unfortunately, we all live in our bodies. And I believe we all deserve to live comfortably, in a pain-free way, in our bodies. I will have to learn how to exercise in a way that is doable. I like this challenge because it fits in with my desire to find sustainable solutions to all of life's problems. Now life is giving me this opportunity to unravel the riddle of how to motivate myself to exercise. It occurs to me that, perhaps, this will be a case of needing to unlearn some ideas that I've picked up about exercise along the way.

Chapter 23

One Moment of Serene and Confident Life

What a divine predicament I'm in. If I don't exercise I'll continue to have balance issues. If I do exercise I can build new neural networks (a prime example of neural plasticity) but first I have to overcome a fear that I'll get dizzy and fall down. I recognize that I'm at yet another crossroads.

I imagine being in the position of being blind and having to wrestle with the choice between staying inside and playing it safe or going out into the world where I will undoubtedly trip and fall or be smacked in the head with a low hanging branch. Do I play it safe? Or do I take a risk?

Life coach Martha Beck reminds us that fear is generated by the reptilian brain, and she goes on to ask, "Do you really want to take advice from a reptile?" This poignant yet comical reminder is just what I need to propel me out into the world.

About a hundred feet from my front door is an idyllic little pond. I estimate that it is about the size of a quarter-mile track and I calculate that if I walk around it four times that would be about one mile so I decide to cultivate a daily habit of walking.

I begin walking around my pond but this time I am not rushing through the walk in a goal-oriented way. Instead I take the time to deeply observe nature. I see this as an opportunity to have my own Walden Pond experience, like Thoreau. The experience is instantly rich and meaningful. I remember back to an idea from Thoreau that has stayed with me, "Bravery deals not so much in resolute action, as in healthy and assured rest ... one moment of serene and confident life is more glorious than a whole campaign of daring."

I begin imagining that I could write a book of my own called, "Everything I Ever Needed to Learn I Learned from My Pond." The first lesson that I learn is about changing my vantage point. Initially I had been a bit disappointed by the view of the pond. While the pond was beautiful, if you looked at it head-on you could see the back of an elementary school with its heating and air conditioning units. The wonderful thing that I quickly discovered, though, was that if I went just a quarter turn around the pond, the view was an exquisite one of gently rolling hills and meadows filled with wildflowers. It was the same pond in the same location but my vantage point was different. I wondered how many other situations in life could benefit from a slight change in perspective?

I make it something of a game for myself to try to notice something different each trip around. I stop and notice the Queen Anne's lace flowers and their beauty seems to touch all the way down to my soul. I remember that Queen Anne's Lace is also called wild carrot and so I sometimes pull one up and smell the wonderful familiar carrot smell of the root and drift into a deeply remembered state of wonder—the same wonder I felt as a child.

I don't think there can be anything more healing than to spend time in nature. I stop and gently caress and admire and smell the flowers. I let ladybugs climb on my fingers and watch spiders industriously spinning their webs. I feel the wind and the sun on my skin and I take time to lie directly on the earth and feel its vastness. I remember once again that we are on a great sphere that is spinning through space at an amazing speed, yet through the miracle of gravity everything appears still. And I actually take the time to watch the clouds roll by.

My four times around the pond gradually progress to six times, then eight, and finally twelve or sixteen. Each journey around sends me into a state of keener observation. I never become bored. I'm diving deep into this experience and reveling at its potential to enlighten. At times I intersperse my walking with a stop for push-ups or tai chi or yoga. I follow my body's own wisdom and it shows me what to do next.

The founder of the Amrit method of yoga, Amrit Desai, spoke about this point of awakening in one's yoga practice, "At this stage, everything you have learned from books, traditions, techniques, and authorities about formal yoga postures ... has to be dropped. From this point on, there is only one book you will read for your practice of yoga—the book of your body." I see that this advice applies to all areas of my life as well. I'm learning to drop everything I've learned, from everywhere, on every topic.

I am unraveling my life as I synthesize a new way for me to be. And I'm reminded of a similar sentiment expressed by architect Nader Kahlili, after he stopped for a vision quest. "Midway through my life I stopped racing with others. I picked up my dreams and began a gentle walk." As my fiftieth birthday approaches this seems like the right time for me to pick up my dreams. But what are my dreams?

As I contemplate this, I know it's time for me to dream a new dream for myself. I have been trained as a therapist but as Dr. Martin Seligman stated in his 1999 speech after becoming president of the American Psychological Association, "The most important thing we learned was that psychology was half-baked, literally half-baked. We've baked the part about mental illness, about repair and damage. The other side's unbaked, the side of strength, the side of what we're good at."

I've also studied coaching (or the "side of what we're good at") and have been trained as a fitness trainer. Somehow none of these disciplines exactly fit. They feel like a pair of shoes that are too tight and I'm feeling a strong need to start walking barefoot. It's time for me to connect with the earth and my own body's wisdom. It's time for me to walk my own walk, and talk my own talk.

Chapter 24

A Re-Visioning

I am now in the process of revising my thinking about exercise. It is a re-visioning. I realize that this shattering I've been through has left me in an ideal place to unlearn some of the unhealthy habits I've learned along the way, and some of these habits are clearly habits of thinking. In Western culture it's obvious that we value action over inaction, busyness over stillness, and effort over ease.

No wonder that the average, over-worked American can't muster up the energy to go and do a "work out" after work. How much energy can we constantly put out? I remember back to times in my twenties when I used to take a step-aerobics class. I think to myself that if I had as much energy to expend as the class required that I wouldn't need a class because I would already be in fantastic shape.

I will have to find a way to ease into fitness. There will be no more artificially stimulating myself with caffeine or psychologically pumping myself up. No more trying to whip myself into shape through bouts of self-loathing that result in classic New Year's resolutions. No more rounds of overdoing it followed by inevitable relapse into old habits followed by disappointment.

As I settle into my new home and my new life, I contemplate ease and new worlds seem to open up to me. Ease is obviously the antidote to dis-ease. I remember something I heard from the Indian sage, Krishnamurti, "Being well-adjusted to a sick society is not a sign of sanity." I wonder how many years it's been that I've been stuck on the hamster wheel of overworking and over-striving?

The practice of yoga and tai chi call to me but I find myself carrying some of the same attitudes into the practice, such as, "I need to be disciplined." The work ethic has permeated every aspect of my thinking and I approach these ancient forms with the classic Western mindset. I can see that I'm not the only one who has fallen into this trap.

Easing into fitness—I take this on as my mantra and open myself up to find a back door into exercise that is not work or discipline-driven. I take the Buddhist teacher Pema Chodron's advice to "start where you are," and my exploration begins with an audible sigh. I deeply exhale and release. And then a phenomenal thing happens—I inhale. Just as day follows night, and night follows day— the deeper I exhale, the deeper I inhale. I am re-discovering my breathing. It is both relaxing and energizing me.

As I gently sigh and release with deep exhalations, I feel a natural impulse to rock back on the floor in the yogic tradition of spinal rocking. Something marvelous and unexpected is happening. I begin tapping into an innate, physical memory of joy. It's as though all the times I flung myself backwards as a child are all stored in my body. I'm realizing that it appears to be the counter-move to sorrow. In crippling grief we feel the innate urge to lean our heads over and down, to fall to our knees and bow our head.

But in joy we can reverse this. As I continue my slow spinal rocking, I imagine that I'm a newlywed who is throwing herself wholeheartedly onto a fluffy down bed, or dipping joyously on the dance floor secure in my lover's arms. I am flooded with memories of being a child— laughing with my playmates as we unselfconsciously roll around on our bedroom floors with our sides splitting with laughter. I am sledding down a hill and flinging myself over into the downy snow or rolling down grassy hills without a care in the world. The head-back and neck-out position is the natural position of abandonment. It is worry-free and filled with natural ease.

I begin noticing all the ways we use words to describe our mind-body connection. We might say that someone looks like she has the "weight of the world on her shoulders" or he looks "bent out of shape." Conversely, someone can be "on her toes." And if we were Mary Poppins we'd advise our young charges to keep their "chins up!"

The practice of yoga is being deeply revealed to me as I discover the mental correlates to our physical position. We maintain postures to align our mind. We connect the body to the mind. I've known this intellectually—that Hatha Yoga actually means to link the body to the mind—but now I'm discovering this truth for myself. It's no longer a theory. I'm realizing it. Then I realize what an amazing word "real-ize" is. When we make something real—it is realized. What a real-ization!

I will ease my way into fitness by exhaling. I begin with a sigh and a deep release. I tilt my head back and rock into my own gentle and naturally embedded joy. The deeper I breathe and release, the deeper I inhale, and soon I am arriving at a new wellspring of energy. I ride this energy like a wave and effortlessly channel it into a classically difficult position—the "boat pose." In this yoga posture one's legs, shoulders, arms, and head are all off the floor in a steady abdominal crunch. As I continue to breathe into this pose I am increasingly energized until the pose becomes pleasant and enlivening.

Suddenly an old teaching from Swami Satchidananda comes to the forefront of my consciousness, "Yoga postures are meant to create ease and comfort." While I'm in the middle of this classically difficult pose, I find that sense of ease. What a discovery! In the past I've been so busy striving that I've failed to achieve the purpose of yoga—to find ease and comfort.

After sustaining the pose effortlessly for an extended time, I release and relax. As I breathe deeply into the relaxation I give it equal attention and value. I now understand that this is the key to enjoying a truly holistic relationship with exercise: To view both exertion and ease as a unified whole.

Chapter 25

Birds Flyin' High ...

On October 20th, my birthday, I notice I am filled with contentment. My home is now full of good energy. It's a pleasure to live here. I pause to reflect on how far I've come along on my grieving process and I notice I haven't cried on a regular basis over Bob for months now. There was one time at the Unity church when I heard the song "Autumn Leaves" that I cried. This was one of Bob's favorite songs and he sang it exquisitely. I imagine I will be struck with occasional and unpredictable bouts of crying throughout my life and I accept this as part-and-parcel of loving deeply.

I also notice that the prospect of turning fifty doesn't fill me with any dread—only curiosity. I love getting older and wouldn't trade this time in my life for any other. I am alone but in no way lonely. I have completely given up any notion of dating and now find I have no interest in it. I am my own person and I've begun to treat myself with all the love and care I deserve. I pamper myself by making a special breakfast and I dress up for my own birthday celebration.

Suddenly the doorbell rings which is a bit of a novelty in the country. When I open it, I am greeted by a flower delivery man holding a completely over-the-top bouquet from my sister in Chicago. I can't remember ever loving flowers more than I do in this moment. As I call my sister to thank her, the doorbell rings again, and this time there's a large package that's been left on the steps. When I open it I find that it is the most fragile gift I could ever imagine receiving through the mail—a colorful Galileo thermometer made out of hand-blown glass. On the note from my niece Julie she says she has this thermometer in her office and feels certain it would be something that I would love, too. How grateful I am to be associated with loving a thing of beauty. I will treasure it forever.

Just when I am thinking that this birthday can't get any better, the doorbell rings for a third time. It is a basket of tulip and daffodil bulbs from my son. The rich symbolism in this gift sets my heart aglow. In my new mode of self-appreciation, I take the time to acknowledge that I raised such a caring young man. Parenting was often such a thankless task. About ten years earlier when my son was racing around on his motorcycle smashing into things and breaking various bones I wasn't all that confident in my parenting. But now, like Julie Andrews in the Sound of Music, I think "I must have done something good."

I turn on my new favorite song from my favorite singer, "Birds flyin' high … you know how I feel… Sun in the sky…you know how I feel" And I think to myself, Yes, I know how it feels!

Chapter 26

✦

A Joyful Noise
unto the Lord

In November, I welcome the opportunity to participate in a Prayer Chaplain training through the new Unity church that I've joined. Our teachers are a wonderful couple, Ned and Constance, who are both in their seventies and extremely devoted to prayer. Constance spends a significant portion of her day knitting prayer shawls for people undergoing surgery. She infuses each stitch of the shawl with a healing intention and by the time she's finished the shawls are alive with a field of pulsating, healing love.

The Chaplain training is guided by a booklet *Come Apart for Awhile* written by Reverends' Janet and Robert Ellsworth and based on Jesus' teachings on prayer. Our program emphasizes that Jesus taught a powerful form of prayer that engages our lives by "uplifting our consciousness." As we delve into the nature of prayer we are encouraged to see that we actually pray more than we may realize. We explore these forms of prayer: 1) Feeling "awed by the beauty in nature;" 2) Feeling "at one with everything around" us; 3) Speaking "words of love and caring;" 4) Finding "spiritual meaning in coincidences;" and 5) Entering "the silence."

Jesus understood that to renew himself he needed to "draw apart" and so he often went alone up into the hills to pray. As his disciple Paul wrote, "Be ye transformed by the renewing of your mind." (Romans 12:2) As I turn to the Bible for inspiration, I am repeatedly drawn to this passage "Trust in the Lord with all your heart and lean not on your own understanding; in all ways acknowledge Him, and He will direct your paths." (Proverbs 3:5-6)

"Lean not on your own understanding." I love this idea and I know that my mind is being truly renewed through my immersion in Stillness where I take the time to listen to the "still, small voice." (1 Kings 19:12) The Christian mystic Meister Eckhart wrote that "Divinity is an underground river that no one can stop and no one can dam up." And Matthew Fox built on this idea in his book *One River, Many Wells*, saying, "There is one underground river—but there are many wells into that river: an African well, a Taoist well, a Buddhist well, a Jewish well, a Muslim well, a goddess well, a Christian well, and aboriginal wells. Many wells but one river."

He goes on to warn that "To go down a well is to practice a tradition but we would make a grave mistake (an idolatrous one) if we confused the well itself with the flowing waters of the underground river." Meister Eckhart's description of Divinity as an underground river reminds me of a dream I once had. I dreamt that I was working in a beautiful temple and there was a bookshelf in the temple. I thought to myself that if I could only take one of the books down from the shelf and read the title then I would really know **the** book to read. I reached for the book and read the cover. It said, **Main Source Wellspring.**

Both within the dream, and upon awakening, I deeply understand that I am connecting with God directly. It's time for me to stop studying religion and let my life become a religion. I express this sentiment in a short bio that I am asked to write about myself for the Unity newsletter to introduce the new Chaplains. I write that I am dedicated to living my "life as a prayer."

In the bio, I also take the opportunity to reinvent myself and say that I am interested in working with people who "don't like to exercise" to help them "fall in love with fitness." At this point I don't know exactly what this will look like but I follow my calling to write it anyway. To my amazement, I immediately get three clients. I am honest about not knowing exactly where I am going and my clients all seemed fine with it. Apparently they recognize my enthusiasm and want to join in my authentic journey of self-discovery.

I know from my love of etymologies that the word enthusiasm contains the root words "en Theo" meaning "with God." I understand that I am, in fact, with God. And we all are with God anytime we do something that we love. My new clients are all good sports and let me try out different approaches with them. It's a combination of physical movement with counseling. Some things work and some things don't but we have a good time along the way.

It isn't until I spontaneously offer to work with one of my new neighbors that I come into my own. Maggie is a simple down-to-earth woman who is a self-proclaimed "hillbilly." She told me she had been born and raised right in North Carolina and that was all she knew. I met her one time when I stopped at her house to inquire about her roof as I was hoping to get a similar roof put on my new home. She invited me in and I chatted with her and her husband all afternoon. Every once in awhile I would say,

"Well, I better be going because I don't want to keep you any longer" and they would heartily protest. We spent a grand afternoon laughing together and developing a lovely bond of friendship

From that point on, Maggie would often stop by to invite me out for a walk where we would enjoy nature and our love of God together. She also loved the way I took care of myself. One day she stopped by and I began spontaneously teaching her some yoga postures. I did this in a very hands-on approach. I guided her body into comfortable positions as I encouraged her to deeply exhale. While she was in a pose I gave her little massages to help her relax into it. As I work with her she is singing my praises about how much better she feels. I intuitively know that I am onto something as I synthesize a new hands-on way of working that seems to incorporate all the best from counseling, coaching, and a new womanly way of self-empowerment.

The next day after I return home from running some errands I find a large package on my front steps. When I open the package, I am astonished to find a three foot high, carved wooden bear that Maggie is offering me as a gift for working with her. I immediately recognize this bear as my animal totem and I understand that I have found my own power. I have followed my bear totem to Hendersonville and now I am receiving confirmation that I am becoming one with my own inner authority.

I have successfully cast off a deeply entrenched taboo about touching clients that I have been indoctrinated with through years of training. I will reject the no-touch taboo as indicative of a society that has lost its natural way. Carla Hannaford, PhD, author of *Smart Moves: Why Learning is Not All in Your Head* states it this way, "It's time to relearn appropriate supportive touch and value it for its function…" Her research clearly shows that "Whenever touch is combined with the other senses, much more of the brain is activated, thus building more complex nerve networks and tapping into more learning potential."

As I breathe deeply, I will sync up my client's breath with my own. I will add gentle supportive touch to create new positive associations with exercise as pleasurable rather than work-oriented. And I will surround us in a field of joyful prayer. We will learn to move our bodies as un-self-consciously as a bird sings, and our sighs will become a "joyful noise unto the Lord." (Psalm 98:4)

Chapter 27

Thanks-Giving

I am filled with a festive spirit as the holidays approach. I actually have time to send cards, and presents, and each act of remembrance fills me with gratitude. I accept the open invitation to share a Thanksgiving dinner at the Unity church and I fend off any sense of self-pity that occasionally wants to creep into my thinking. Rather than create a sad-story that I will tell myself about how I have nowhere to go for Thanksgiving dinner, I decide that I will enjoy the offer I do have.

I am reminded of a time when I had to work on Christmas day in the psychiatric ward of a hospital as

I was completing my counseling internship. A friend of mine surprised me by showing up with his guitar to sing to the patients. It turns out that he was a regular volunteer and he told me that he volunteered every Christmas at the hospital. It was clear that he was as happy as a clam and he made a world of difference that day for the patients and staff alike.

I remember being deeply impressed by my friend's spirit and commitment to joy. It is so evident that it is in giving that we receive. I can't help but imagine that if all the people who are feeling sorry for themselves somewhere in the world would actually pick themselves up and decide to help someone else how much better the world would be. I decide that I will show up at the church dinner and be there for others too.

It isn't difficult to share joy at the Unity Thanksgiving dinner. In fact, it turns out to be the best Thanksgiving of my life! Whatever is wonderful about a family dinner is amplified to the power of ten at Unity. The sanctuary had been transformed into a dazzling banquet hall with linen-covered tables and flower centerpieces. There are at least three hundred fun-loving people present with sumptuous tables filled with every possible variation on a dish. I've brought a cornbread stuffing made with chestnuts and apricots to add to the twenty other offerings of stuffing.

And instead of one pumpkin pie there are tables of them, each one looking more delicious than the next.

After a meal that nourishes our hearts as much as our bodies we are treated to a repeat performance of some of the "Unity Does Broadway" favorites: such as "How to Handle a Woman" from Camelot and "If Momma was Married" from Gypsy. After the show tunes, the stage is opened up for open-mic performances. My favorite performer is a shy fellow who can barely talk but when he opens his mouth to sing he brings down the house with his soulful country singing. I can't help but do some hootin' and hollerin' as he sings and I didn't even know I had any hootin' and hollerin' in me.

I am having such a good time that I actually pass on the dessert table. Then to my happy surprise, I am invited over to a new friend's house to continue the fun for desserts. It turns out that we are all new to the area and are all equally appreciative of the opportunity to share the holiday with new friends. We all stay late into the night playing one of those games where you make up silly definitions to obscure words from the dictionary. I have the sense that my dance partners are changing but the same beautiful dance of life is still going on.

Chapter 28

Every Cloud has a Silver Lining

Over the Christmas holidays, I fly to San Diego to spend some time with my son Jared. It has been almost a year since we have seen each other. Last February, immediately after Bob's memorial service, I had taken the train down to be with him. When Jared met me at the station he put his arm around me and said, "You lean on me now, Mom, and we'll get through this together." At that moment I witnessed my son fully become his own man.

It makes perfect sense that a child would come into his own in response to a crisis but it's something I had never thought about before. This was another unexpected gift of the mourning process. It reminded me of the saying that "every cloud has a sliver lining." In my weakened state, my son's full strength came into being. Now almost a year later I can revel in his newly discovered power. What a pleasure this is to me. I remember when he was a baby being deeply impressed by a teaching to treat a baby as a baby when they are young—so that as an adult they can be an adult.

The wisdom of that statement stayed with me and I always kept it as my guiding principle in parenting. I would allow my son to fully experience each stage of his life—both to enjoy it and to be ready to put the things of childhood behind him when he was an adult. How many adults in the world are really nothing but overgrown children? They have never fully concluded their stages of development. Judith Viorst adeptly addressed this idea in her book, *Necessary Losses: The Loves, Illusions, Dependencies and Impossible Expectations that all of us Have to Give Up in Order to Grow.* She writes, "These losses are a part of life—universal, unavoidable, inexorable. And these losses are necessary losses because we grow by losing and leaving and letting go."

At six foot four inches, my son is not only fully grown physically but he is also his own man with a big, generous, and loving heart. My son is man enough to show his affection for me without any sense of self-consciousness too. On Christmas day we go to the Coronado peninsula. Jared holds my hand as we walk down the street and I can't help but to notice that all the middle-aged women we pass all break out into big approving smiles. I don't think they could be sure whether this was a mother with a very loving son or an older woman with a younger man—but either way they like it!

To be honest, I blushed a bit while simultaneously marveling at my son's own independent nature. That day had a dream-come-true quality to it. It's an ideal seventy-two degrees with ocean breezes blowing gently. We rent a bicycle-built-for-two and ride up and down the beach and all around the peninsula enjoying all the whimsical California Christmas decorations—things like surfing Santas and hip reindeer. We drink hot chocolate and watch ice skaters in an outdoor rink next to the ocean. But enjoying the man my son has become feels like the ultimate dream come true.

Chapter 29

❦

Petitionary Prayer

My flight to visit my son in San Diego has been such a breeze that I board the plane home with no trepidation whatsoever. About two hours into the flight, however, I hear an announcement that is my worst fear made manifest. The captain comes over the loudspeaker to announce that we are in for several hours of turbulence and that unfortunately there is no way around it. Additionally, he notes that the flight attendants will need to be buckled in and will not be available to answer any distress calls.

With my balance disorder, getting dizzy remains a very real problem for me. Certain things trigger this and flying is one of the worst culprits. I shut my eyes, clutch the armrests on my seat, and within seconds the bumpy ride begins. At this moment, I truly believe that I would prefer death to this and I have to hold myself back from praying that we will crash just to get it over with.

While I had learned to expand my understanding of prayer during my chaplain training, I quickly revert back to the basic petitionary style; "Oh God please, please, please, help me. Oh God please." I squirm in my seat while inwardly screaming in silent anguish. This is my worst nightmare come true. I know that all my fellow passengers are going through the same thing and I will have to weather this storm on my own.

My begging and pleading prayers turn into attempted deal-making with God. As the plane bumps and lurches along, I am thrown this way and that like a rag doll. This continues for a solid hour. Gradually my hysteria begins to abate as I appear to run out of steam to fuel it and I am able to be a bit more in sync with the relentless bouncing, the way I imagine a horseback rider learns to relax into the process of riding a horse.

Eventually, I manage to calm down enough to accept the unpredictable drops and bumps and rolls without crying. After an hour and a half, I have the sensation that I am on a crazy massage chair that works you over real good. At the two hour point, I have mysteriously adapted and find the whole experience relaxing. Of course, I can't help but notice that nothing has changed except my reaction to it. When I had perceived it as my worst nightmare coming true—it was. When I perceive it as relaxing with nothing to worry about—it is.

As abruptly as it started it stopped and the last hour of our flight is as smooth as silk. After the plane lands and we are walking down the boarding ramp to the terminal, I overhear a toddler ask his mother, "Can we do it again?" I laugh to myself and have the distinct feeling that God is laughing too.

Chapter 30

Adagio

After the holidays pass with so much gaiety, I can't help but to be amazed at how far I've come. I think of Bob with gratitude rather than sorrow. In fact, his memory brings an involuntary smile to my whole being. Then January rolls round and I find myself spiraling back down into a deep vortex of sorrow. As the anniversary of Bob's passing approaches, I am consumed with longings for him and I feel like I'm being swallowed alive.

This time I'm reluctant to go back into the sorrow. I have been on such a long road to come out of it that I don't want to go back in. Despite my conscious reluctance to return to the mourning process, I find myself irresistibly drawn to the quintessential piece of music to epitomize human suffering, Samuel Barber's "Adagio for Strings." It's probably been the musical sound track for more tragic movie moments than any other single piece of music in history. I surrender to its dark appeal and listen to it over and over again.

I now have to admit to myself that I am somehow enjoying this pain. The pain is so intrinsically tied to the love I feel that to give it up feels like I am giving up my connection to Bob. I can imagine my life spread out before me as one continuous state of mourning. The process that I have honored—and even celebrated—now has a hold on me that feels like quicksand. I'm both afraid to stay in and I'm afraid to get out and I feel like such a coward. How ashamed I am of these feelings. But, in truth, I've become like an addict who is addicted to my own sorrows.

It's painful to admit that I want to stay in the hurting and I want to stay stuck because I will do anything to stay with Bob. Even though our love was all about life and living, I am in serious danger of never breaking free. I understand intellectually that this makes no sense but I can't seem to stop myself. As I ride this emotional roller coaster, I have no idea how this story will end. All I know is that I have been blindly groping along as I go.

Chapter 31

The Grace that Blesses

As the actual date of Bob's passing approaches, I have a deep desire to share this anniversary with friends. What a gift it would be if I could express my love for Bob through a sharing circle. I want to talk about him and show pictures and play his music. Perhaps not surprisingly, however, most of my new friends wriggled out of my invitation with the merciful exception of two intrepid souls, Golda and Sam.

Golda went even further and said that in the Jewish tradition, the year of mourning is drawn to a close through prayers and a ritual. She offers to lead me in such a ritual. Her offer is one of those life-affirming moments that I recognize immediately. I reach out to respond to her offer with all the desperation of a drowning child. "Yes!" I plead with her, "Please, please help me!"

I understand that I need to end this. To continue mourning indefinitely would be to dishonor my life and the fact that I am still living. I knew that it had taken courage to go into the mourning process but I never would have anticipated that it would take courage to come out as well. Therefore, our little gathering of three is incredibly precious to me. After I play a recording of Bob singing "When You Wish upon a Star" and tell stories, I share some of my favorite photographs and it feels like a very happy occasion. When I am finished, Golda recites some prayers in Hebrew and sings. It's like hearing a mass in Latin. My conscious mind can't follow along—yet my soul deeply understands.

I follow her prayers by giving voice to my own intention to bring this year of mourning to an end. It is time. I will embrace myself and I will embrace the rest of my life. As I do this I can feel the promise of my future—pregnant with so many possibilities—as I step across the energetic threshold to walk into it. And just like that—it is finished.

I know I am complete. I have never even heard of such an idea before. Yet I recognize the wisdom in it. As Richard Heinburg, author of *Celebrate the Solstice* writes, "If you're really ready to complete the cycle or pattern that has been running your life for months or even years, do what you can to establish closure and release the situation with grace in your heart." He goes on to write, "That sense of grace will be the energy that blesses the conception of your next situation." And as Christian mystic Meister Eckhart observed, "Only those who dare to let go, dare to re-enter."

Both the ancient wisdom traditions and a study of nature contain the know-how to help us navigate through life's "inevitable ups and downs." The cycles of life are played out for us over and over again. All we have to do is pay attention. As Florida Scott-Maxwell wrote, "Life does not accommodate you; it shatters you." But lest we lose heart, she puts into words the obvious truth that we all tend to ignore: "Every seed destroys its container, or else there would be no fruition." When I first started this journey into mourning, I could never have anticipated it would end with an understanding of its beauty—but now I do. At last, I see beauty everywhere.

Afterword

I would be remiss if I didn't include an afterword about the way my mourning process continues. Something unexpected will trigger me and the floodgates will open wide. I spiral back into cycles of grief and I go through the whole process again and again. These excursions back into deep sorrow do not discourage me. Instead, I view them as sacred journeys to be mined for their treasures and I welcome the opportunity to keep my "grief glistening" and to "cry easily like a little child." And, dear reader, I encourage you to do the same.

Bibliography

Al Huang, Chungliang, and Jerry Lynch. *Working Out, Working Within: The Tao of Inner Fitness Through Sports and Exercise.* New York: Jeremy P. Tarcher/Putnam Books, 1998.

Barks, Coleman. *Delicious Laughter: Rambunctious Teaching Stories from the Mathnawi.* Athens, GA: Maypop Books, 1990.

Beck, Martha. *Finding Your Own North Star: Claiming the Life You Were Meant To Live.* New York, NY: Three Rivers Press, 2001.

Campbell, Joseph. *The Hero With a Thousand Faces.* Princeton, NJ: Princeton University Press, 1968.

Chodron, Pema. *Start Where You Are: A Guide to Compassionate Living.* Boston, MA: Shambala Publications, Inc., 1994.

Covey, Stephen. *Seven Habits of Highly Effective People: Powerful Lessons in Personal Change.* New York, NY: Free Press, 1989.

Desai, Yogi Amrit. *Kripalu Yoga: Meditation-In-Motion. Book II Focusing Inward.* Lenox, MA: Kripalu Publications, 1985.

Ellsworth, Reverend Janet B. M.S. and Reverend Robert B. Ellsworth, Ph.D. *Come Apart For Awhile: Four Ways to Pray Taught By Jesus.* Bend OR: Thriving Churches Ministry, 1995.

Fox, Matthew. *One River, Many Wells.* New York: University Press of America, 1989.

Garner, Mary. *The Hidden Souls of Words: Keys to Transformation Through the Power of Words.* New York, NY: Select Books, Inc., 2004.

Hannaford, Carol, Ph.D. *Smart Moves: Why Learning is Not All In Your Head.* Arlington, Virginia: Great Ocean Publishers, 1995.

Heinburg, Richard. *Celebrate the Solstice: Honoring the Earth's Seasonal Rhythms Through Festival and Ceremonies.* Wheaton IL: The Theosophical Publishing House, 1993.

Khan, Hazrat Inayat. *Mastery Through Accomplishment: Developing Inner Strength for Life's Challenges.* New Lebanon: Omega Publications, 1993.

Lesser, Elizabeth. *Broken Open: How Difficult Times Help Us Grow.* New York: Villard Books/Random House, 2004.

Loder, Ted. *Guerrillas of Grace: Prayers For the Battle.* Minneapolis, MN: Augsburg Fortress, Publishers. 1984.

McClelland, Carol L. Ph.D. *The Seasons of Change: Using Nature's Wisdom to Grow Through Life's Inevitable Ups and Downs.* Boston MA: Conari Press, 1998.

Moore, Thomas. *Care of the Soul: A Guide For Cultivating Depth And Sacredness In Everyday Life.* New York, NY: Harper Collins Publishers, Inc., 1992.

Oliver, Mary. *Dream Work*. New York, NY: Atlantic Monthly Press, 1986.

Pink, Daniel. *A Whole New Mind: Why Right-Brainers Will Rule the Future*. New York, NY: The Berkley Publishing Group, 2005.

Satchidananda, Yogiraj Sri Swami. *Integral Yoga Hatha*. Yogaville: Integral Yoga Publications, 1995.

Seligman, Martin, Ph.D. *Authentic Happiness: Using the New Positive Psychology to Realize Your Potential for Lasting Fulfillment*. New York, NY: The Free Press, 2002.

Steindl-Rast, Brother David. *Gratefulness, the Heart of Prayer: An Approach to Life in Fullness*. New York: Paulist Press, 1984.

Tolle, Eckhart. *A New Earth: Awakening to Your Life's Purpose*. New York, NY: PLUME/Penguin Group, 2005.

Viorst, Judith. *Necessary Losses: The Loves, Illusions, Dependencies, and Impossible Expectations That All of Us Have to Give Up in Order to Grow*. New York, NY: Fireside, 1986.

Manufactured By: RR Donnelley
                    Breinigsville, PA USA
                    May, 2010